*Commissioned by Margaret Carlaw, Derek Ogston and the sound Festival*

*Dedicated to my dear friend, Professor Derek Ogston C.B.E.,
on the occasion of his 80th birthday*

# CRUCIFIXUS

Six meditations on the prophecy and passion of our Lord

## I: Introit - How beautiful on the mountains

*Dedicated, in memoriam, to Lt. Col. Robert J. Owen*

Based on Isaiah 52:7

PAUL MEALOR

© 2012 Novello and Company Limited

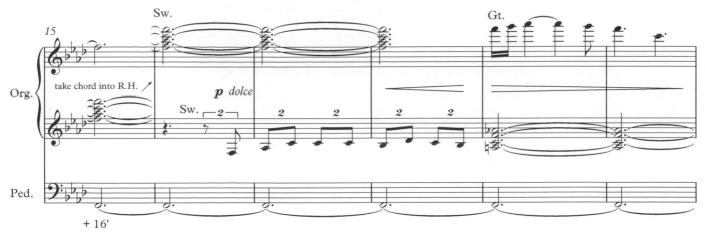

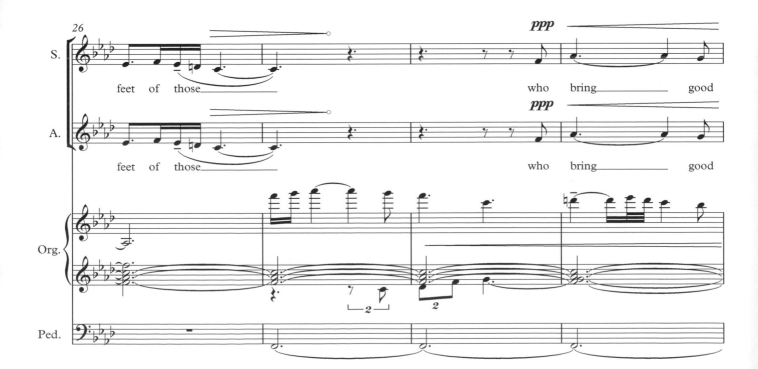

news,_____ who bring good___ news._____

news,_____ who bring good___ news._____

4

How beau-ti-ful on the moun-tains are the feet of those,

6

peace, of peace,_____ and pro - claim the gos - pel of peace._____ Al - le -

* Continue singing these notes in this order, though speed up and/or slow down at will, independently of everyone else. The effect desired is one of a gentle, lilting brook.

moun-tains___ are the feet of those_____ who pro - claim the___ gos-pel of peace.___

*molto rit.*

* Gradually fade away into silence,
each singer stopping independently.

Al - le - lu - ia, al - le - lu - ia.

*Dedicated to Regina Jäschke*

## II: Your silence is stillness

Peter Davidson

Your si - lence is the still - ness be-fore day.

Tronus meus in columna, in flagella para - tus sum, pa-

senza 16', uncoupled, bright, bell-like

-ra - tus _____ sum.

Freely, out of tempo, plainchant

♩ = 48

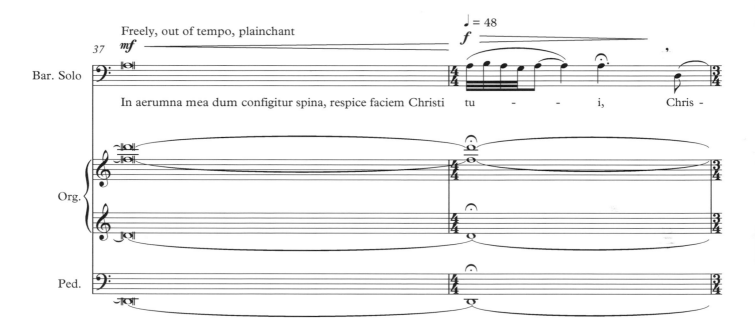

In aerumna mea dum configitur spina, respice faciem Christi tu - i, Chris -

- ti _____ tu - - - - i. _____

*Dedicated to Christopher Bell*
*& The National Youth Choir of Scotland*

# III: O sweetest Jesus

Based on the Roman Catholic
'Prayer before a crucifix'

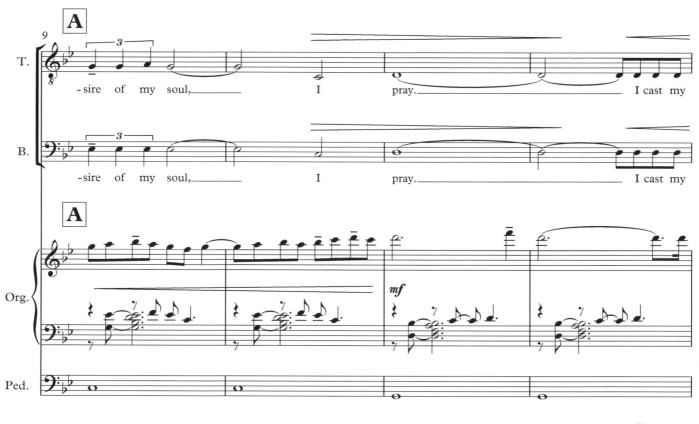

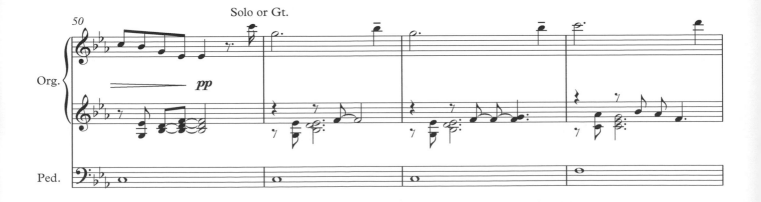

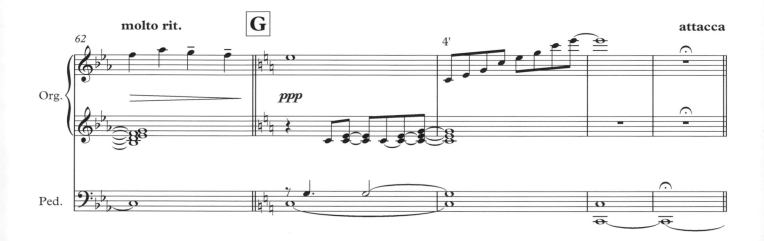

*Dedicated to Joshua Copeland and The Antioch Chamber Ensemble*

# IV: Drop, drop, slow tears

Phineas Fletcher
(1582–1650)

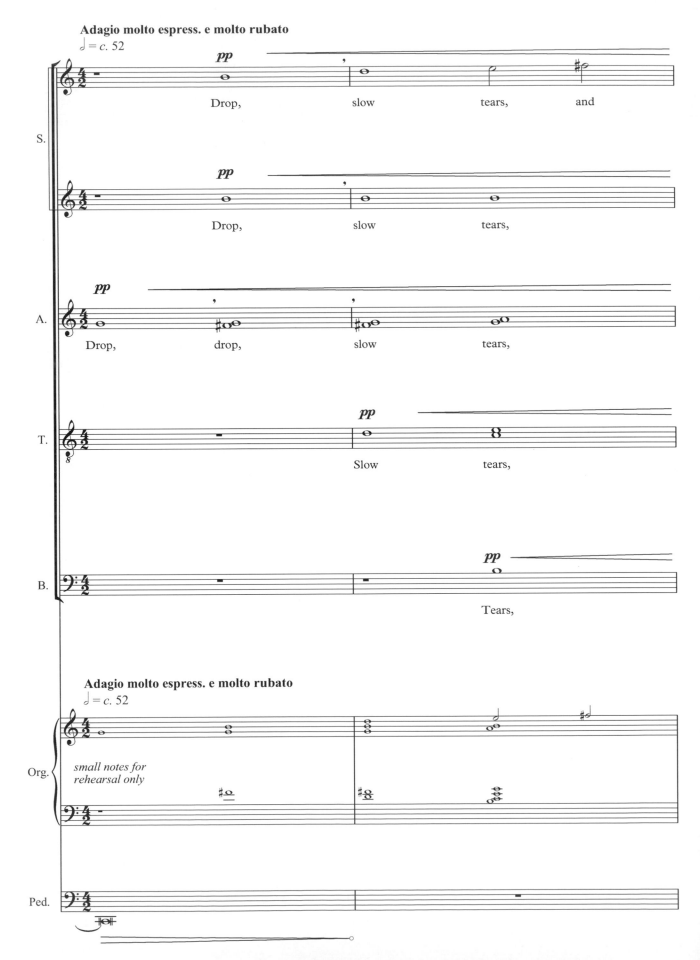

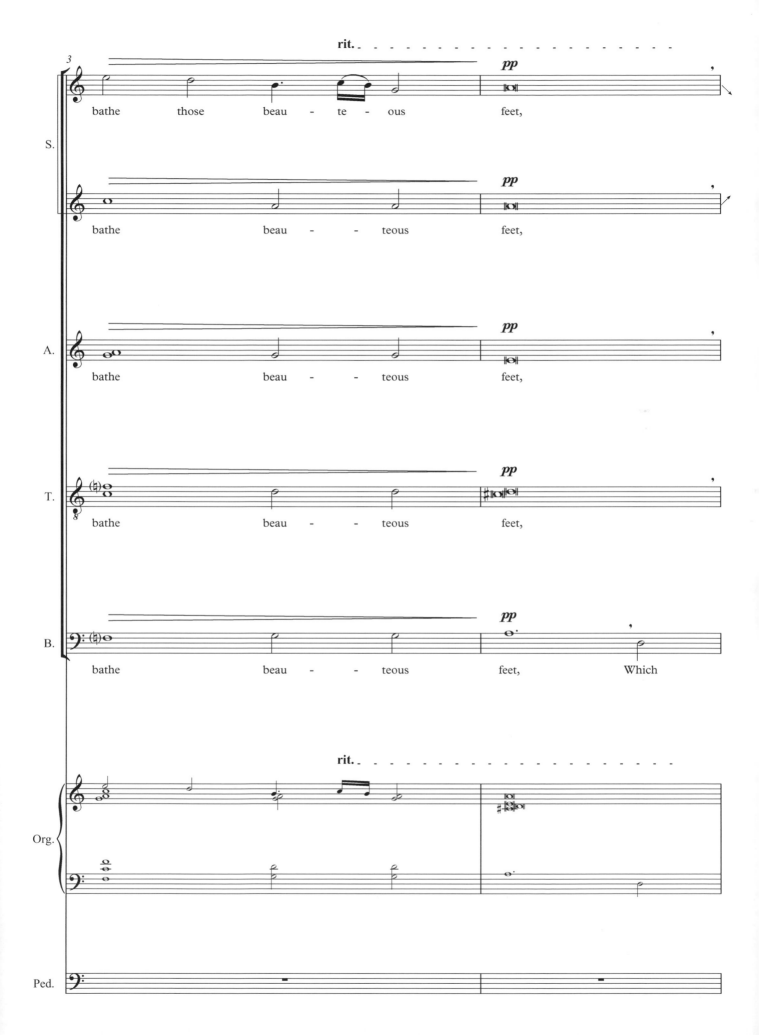

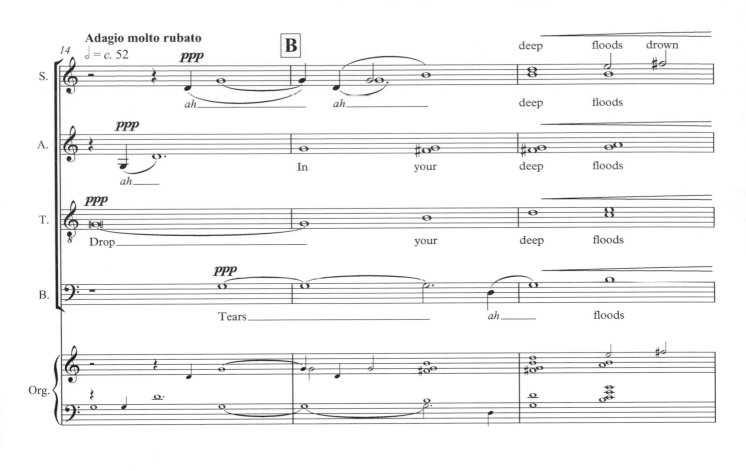

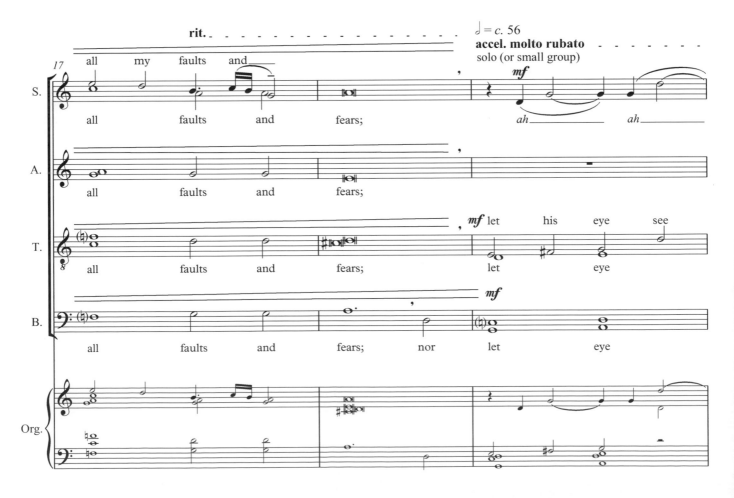

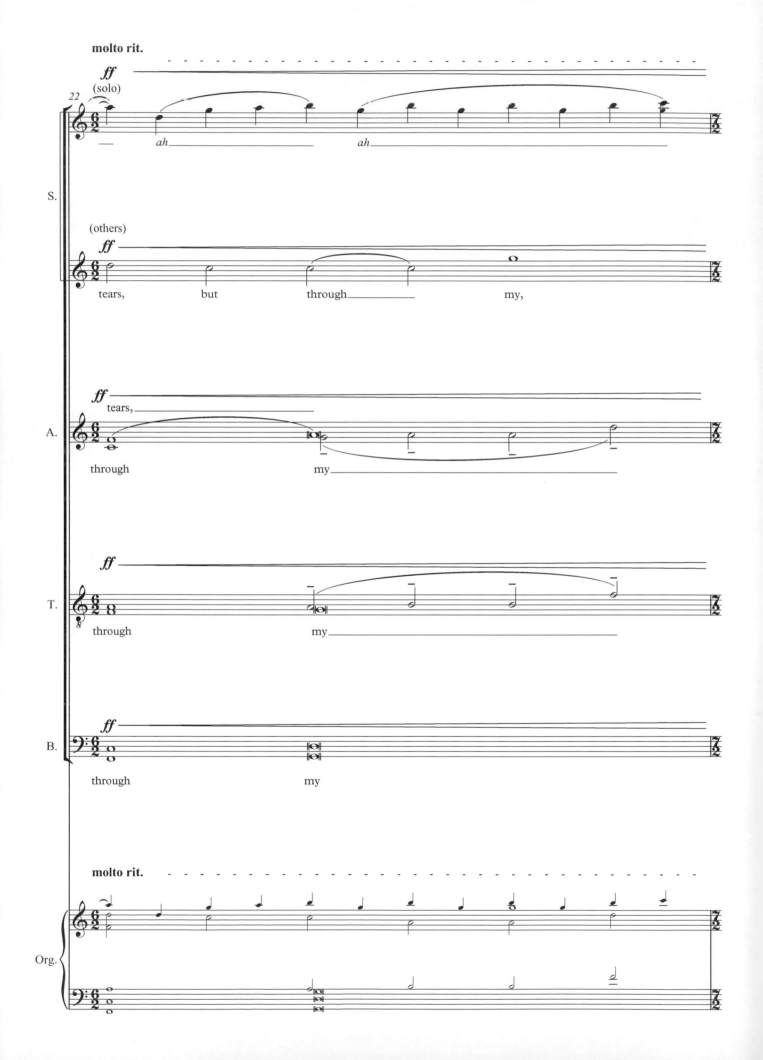

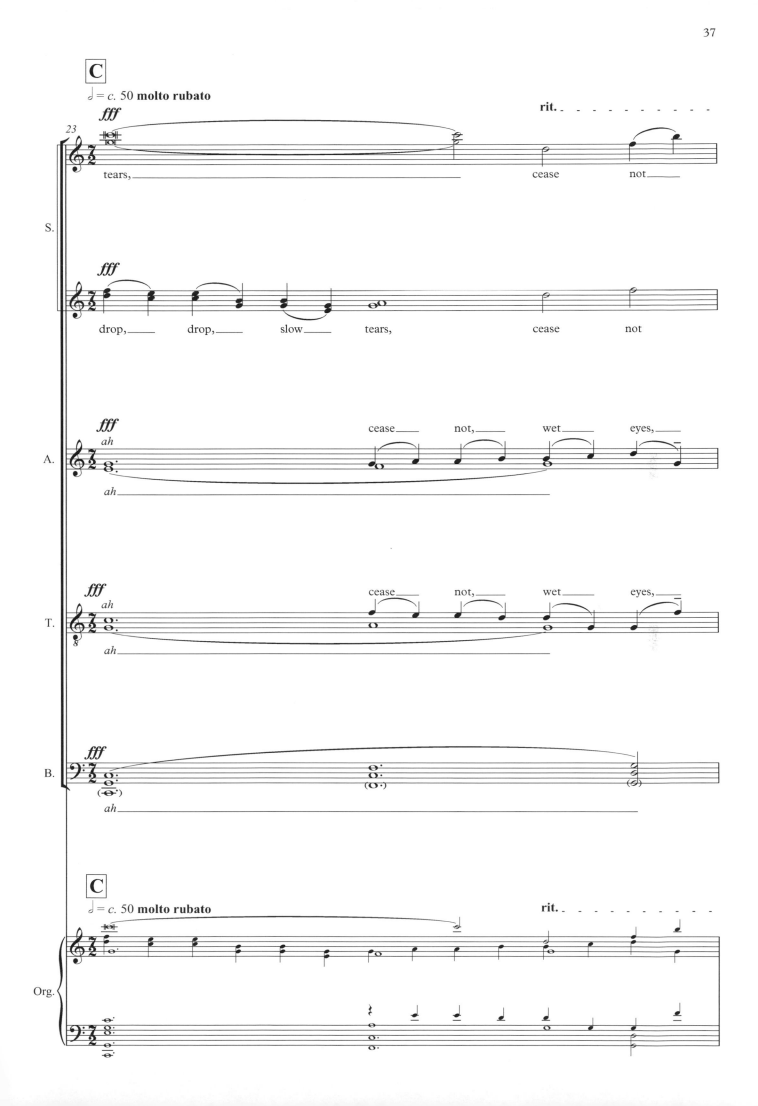

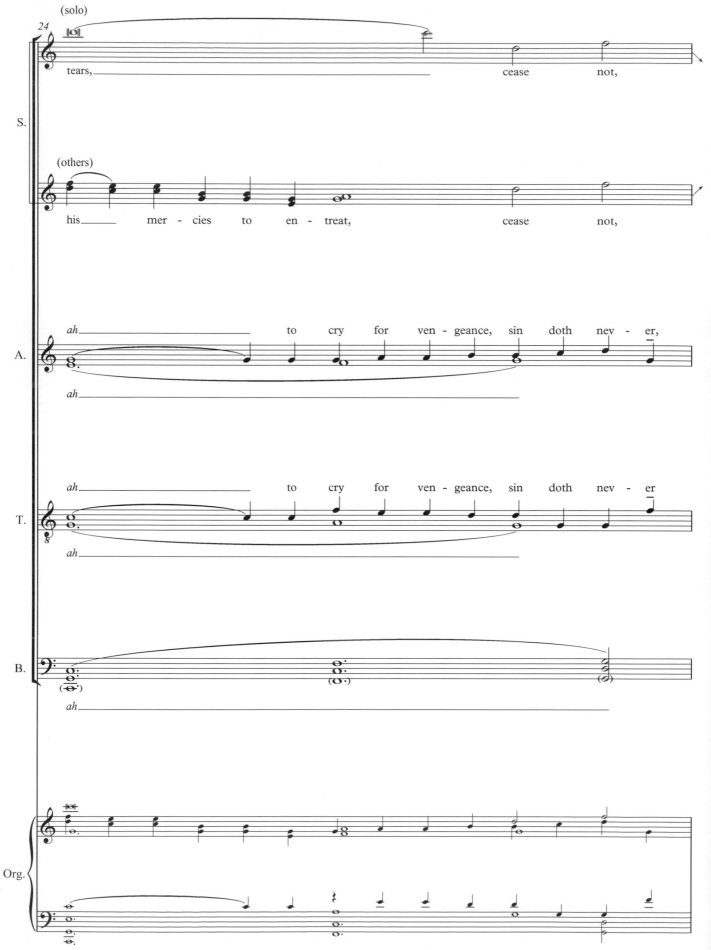

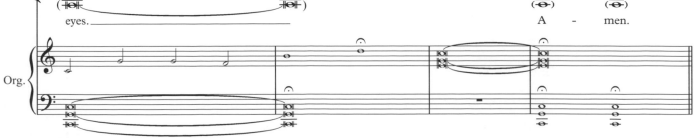

*Dedicated, in memoriam, to Donald Hawksworth*

# V: The tree takes living flame

Peter Davidson

*\* Where part of a word appears in brackets, sing the phrase to the first part of the word finishing it only at the end of the phrase.*

*Dedicated to James Jordan & The Westminster Williamson Voices*

# VI: Finale - I tend you in paradise

Peter Davidson

tend-ed you_____ in pa-ra-dise,_____ my peo-ple,

raised you as_____ the chos-en vine,_____ in

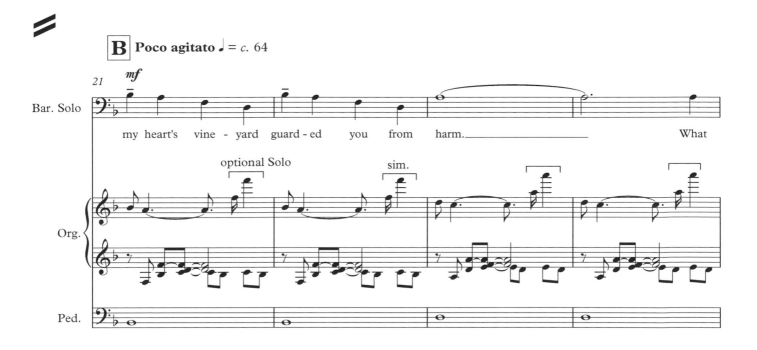

**B** **Poco agitato** ♩ = c. 64

my heart's vine-yard guard-ed you from harm._____ What

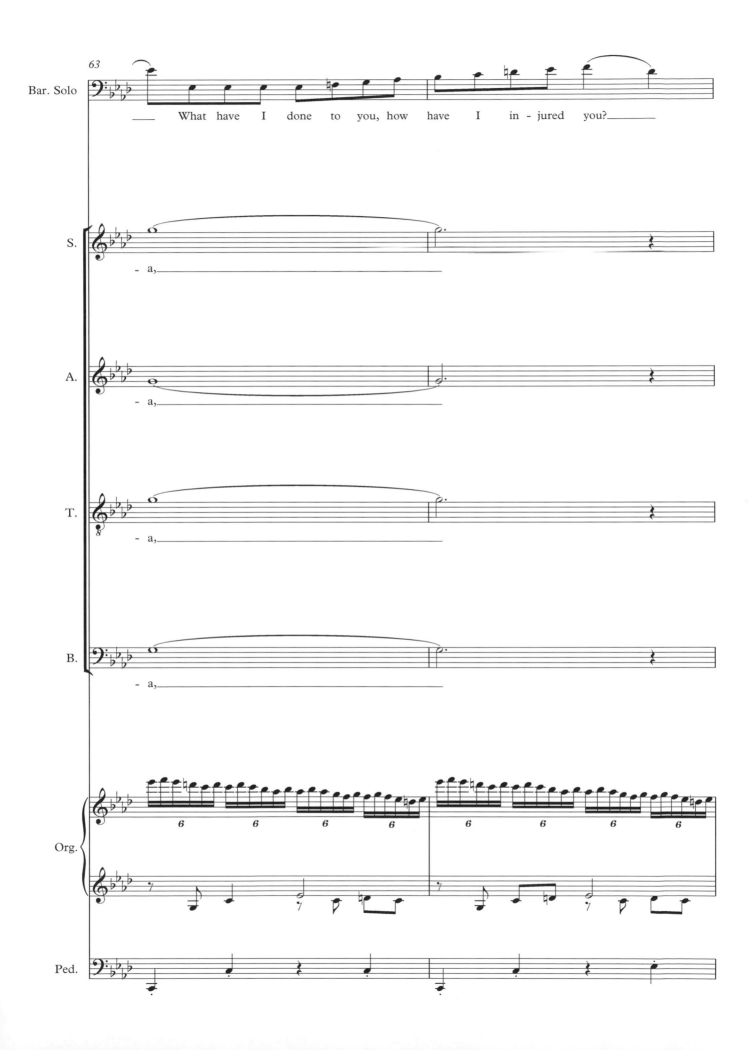

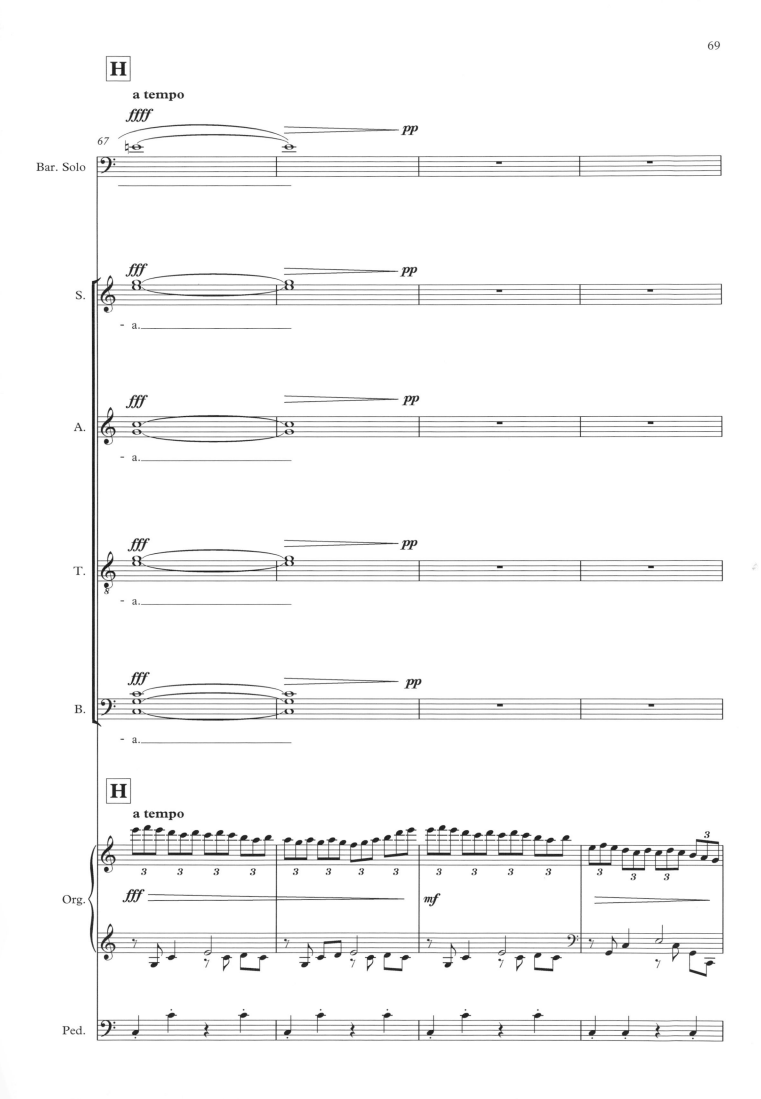

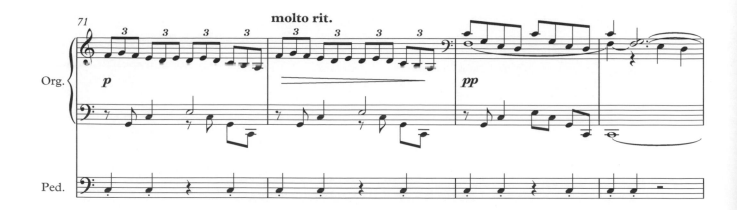

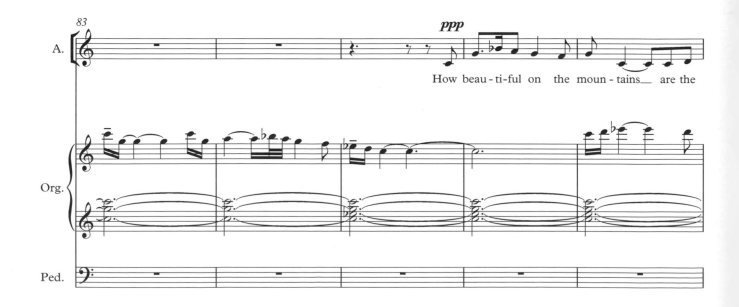

feet of those who bring good news.

*ppp*
Your si - lence is the still-ness be-fore day.

Sw. to Ped., no Ped. stops drawn

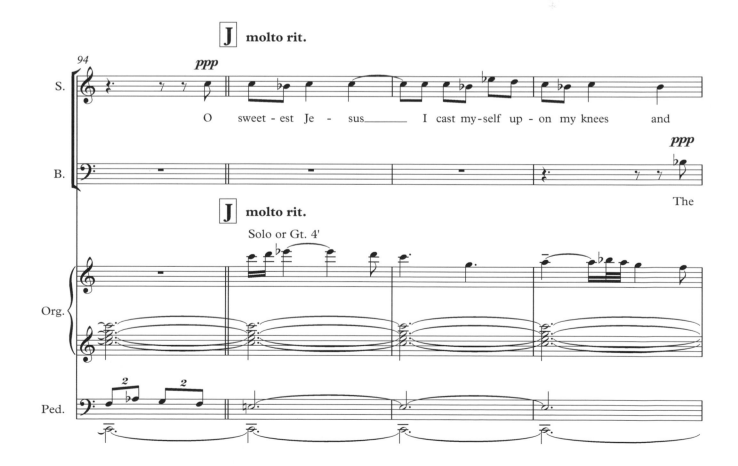

**J** **molto rit.**

*ppp*
O sweet-est Je - sus I cast my-self up - on my knees and

*ppp*
The

**J** **molto rit.**

Solo or Gt. 4'

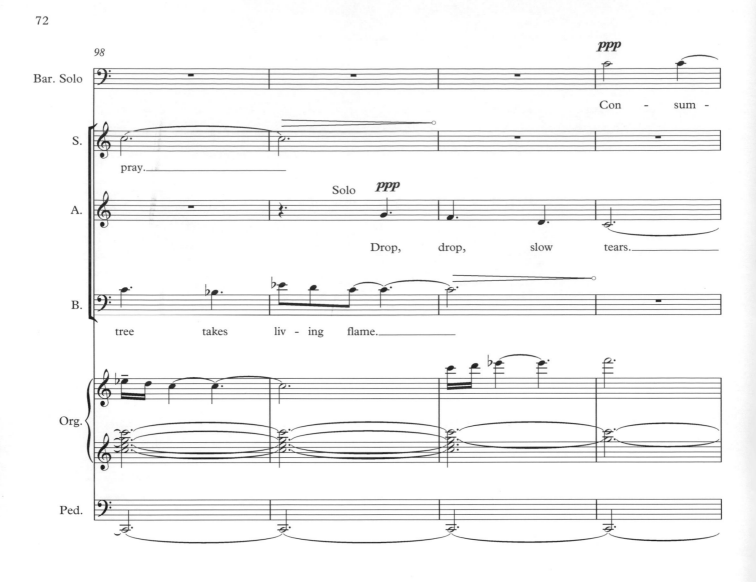

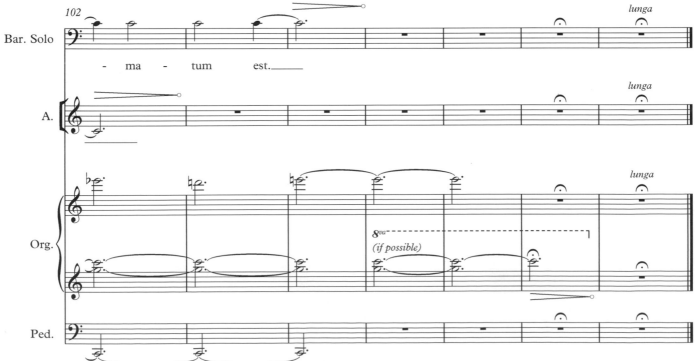